Unlocking the Secrets of Being an Amputee Spouse

Thank you to everyone who has helped us in even the smallest of ways. We are blessed to have met you all.

(in no particular order)

Dylan Whitney, Greyson Whitney, Gabriel Whitney, Caleb Whitney, Bremer Prosthetics team, Dr. Omar Haqqani and Staff, Mid-Michigan Hospital staff, Margo Davies, Duane Davies, Allen and Jill Derocher, Caroline Martin, Martin Whitney, Paula Tullos, Laura McCaig, Maralee Morgan, Sandy Harrington, Lonnie Kramer, Charlotte Kirksey, Dr. Hunter, Dr. Christine Murphy, Diabetes Center Staff, Dr. James Shepich, Mid-Michigan Anticoagulation Clinic Staff, Craig Scott, Dr. Muhammad Jilani, Kristin Johnson, PA, Dr. Jeffrey Stone, Dr. Philip Harris, Dr. Mark Horness, Dr. Subramanyam Yadam, Dr. Thomas Regenbogen, Jeanne Singer, Members of the Caregiver/Spouse of Amputees FB page, Kevin Kappler

Without you all, we would have been lost. Thank you.

Dear readers,

For some time now I have felt a gentle nudge from the universe to write a book about our experience when my husband suffered a medical emergency that changed our lives forever. It has taken me nearly three years to get to a place where I can tell the details without reliving the trauma. Over the past few months I have spent many hours writing down the events that unfolded that fateful June day in 2016 and the many months that were to follow. I painstakingly arranged the details in chronological order. I wrote about how a medical emergency devastated our lives financially, medically, emotionally, and mentally in ways we never could have imagined. I was 45 pages in when I stopped and shoved the whole thing in a drawer to be left unfinished...forever.

It's a great story of life-saving heroics, love, finding untapped strength, overcoming obstacles, and solving medical mysteries. It is a story of strength, courage, and facing our greatest fears. But at the end of the day, it isn't my story to tell. It is Jason's story. It contains intimate details of the stresses he has endured and the battles he has fought. Details that I have no right exposing to the world-at-large. In the end, it would have become a memoir of the worst years of our lives, forever etched in ink. But, at the end of the day, we aren't what happened to us. We are forged from what has happened to us. And that is the story I want to share. I want the world to know that when all seemed lost, we banded together and fought for our lives both figuratively and literally. Maybe more importantly, I want to write for you the handbook I wish I had had...the manual I so desperately needed. So, without further ado, I introduce you to that guide. May it be a helping light when you find yourself surrounded by darkness!

Sincerely,

Sabrina Whitney

Our Story

We were married in the fall of 2003. Jason worked while I
stayed home to care for his two children and our home. In
the spring of 2004 we welcomed our first child together
and four short months later we experienced Jason's first
medical dilemma. Within a few months of being
diagnosed with diabetes, Jason suffered a diabetic coma
when his blood glucose level dropped to 23 while
sleeping. Quick thinking on my part and swift medical
interventions saved his life. To fully recover he would
spend a week in the hospital. The days grew longer as our
daily routine was put aside and our new 'hospital routine'
developed. Every morning I would prepare the older two
boys for school and drop them off. Our four-month old
son and I would then head to the hospital to sit at Jason's
bedside until school ended for the day. At this time, I
would pick up the boys and we would head home. The
boys would change out of their uniforms and do any
homework they had while I prepared a portable dinner.
Once packed up, our gang would drive to the hospital to

eat with Jason and hang out until visiting hours ended. On day seven Jason was released and we fully expected to put the hospital life behind us.

Fast forward eight years to December 2012. His oldest child has reached adulthood and our youngest was a mere three months old. Jason had been experiencing sharp pain in his lower back and butt cheek for some time. His doctor insisted it was sciatica, refused to perform testing, and repeatedly sent him on his way.

We woke early on Christmas morning to open gifts with all of our children and were alarmed to see that Jason's left leg was red and severely swollen. He insisted we open gifts and enjoy breakfast before heading to the hospital, knowing he wouldn't be leaving the hospital until his health issue was sorted out. A one-week long stay and several tests discovered that the pain Jason had been experiencing for all those months was actually not sciatica, as his doctor had insisted, but was instead caused by a blood clot in the vein running the length of his left leg. This clot was many years in the making as it stretched from his groin down to the middle of his shin. The medical staff were able to reduce the swelling and made the decision to treat the clot with prescription blood thinners. One year after his hospitalization, Jason was taken off the blood thinners and was assured by his doctor that 'blood thinners don't dissolve clots they just stop them from getting bigger'. Follow-up tests revealed that the original clot shrank to 1/3 its original size. Despite our requests for answers to how such a large blood clot could have formed and the consequences of having such a significantly sized clot remaining without blood thinner interventions we were told 'sometimes these things just happen' and 'the body will eventually reabsorb the clot, it's what it does'.

We would find ourselves in the emergency room many more times due to overwhelming pain and years would pass before emergency room staff were able to scan his leg without freaking out over the size of his clot. It was a short lived victory though.

By the time 2016 arrived, Jason's pain had increased steadily. He sought relief and answers from his doctor who still claimed it was sciatica even after his history with blood clots. He was offered pain medications and sent on his way again.

At this point Jason was working two jobs at full-time hours, fighting through the pain, in the hopes of saving up enough money to finally buy a house and to begin preparing for retirement. Life had other ideas for us though. Just as in the past, the pain he experienced was not caused by sciatica and did not actually originate where it presented. We would learn this information the hardest way possible on June 11, 2016.

On the evening of June 10th Jason worked an overnight shift for a co-worker. He returned home early the next morning and woke me up to the news that he couldn't feel his right foot and it was ice cold to the touch. Now, June 11th happens to be his birthday, he was turning 47 and he knew that if he went to the hospital for treatment he would be immediately admitted so, we made a deal. He could stay home and celebrate his birthday but he had to go to the hospital for evaluation early the next morning.

On June 12th we walked into the hospital's emergency room. After initial tests revealed a two-inch blood clot in the artery of his right thigh, he was admitted and prepped for surgery. Sure that this was the source of the problem, we were assured that after the clot was removed, blood flow would be restored and Jason would be walking out of the hospital in three days and able to return to work the following week.

The truth was that after the surgery to remove the clot, Jason's pain level soared exponentially. As the hours passed and the pain became intolerable, the doctor's began running more tests.

For those of you not formally trained in human anatomy, we all have an aortic artery that runs down the center of our chest cavity. Just above our belly button this artery splits in two and branches off into each leg. When this arterial branch reaches the knee it splits into three arteries that supply blood to the leg and foot.

This second round of tests revealed that the clot in Jason's thigh was not the only one. All three arteries of his right shin were significantly clotted. The extent wouldn't be known until angioplasty was performed a few days later. This procedure took longer than anticipated because one artery was so blocked that they couldn't enter it and the other two kept re-closing shortly after being cleaned out. Eventually the two arteries were opened and all we could do was hope they would remain that way.

Overall, the angioplasty was considered a success. Jason was on the road to recovery. And a few days later he was sent to a local rehab center for in-patient rehabilitation to regain the muscle strength he lost while being confined to a bed for over a week.

Jason was now entering his third week out of work and our tight budget was getting tighter so he insisted to go to a local rehab facility instead of the out-of-town rehabilitation center recommended by his care team. This would save me time and money visiting him but it came with its own difficulties.

While in this rehab center, Jason noticed a significant increase in his pain level and a slight discoloration of his foot. In a ten-day time span, his foot would turn from flesh color to pink to deep red to a dark purple, bordering on black. The nurse on day duty during his stay told him every day the doctor would be in tomorrow. Tomorrow never brought a doctor with it. On day nine she switched out his narcotic pain killers with Tylenol 3 because she had failed to refill his prescription and had no intentions to do so.

The pain was intense and he begged me to help him the morning of day nine. Until this point, he had only told me of the color changes but refused to show me his foot. At the time I left on day eight, his foot was red. It quickly escalated to dark purple through the night. When I arrived on day nine, as soon as I set everything down, I insisted on looking at his foot. I immediately called his vascular surgeon for an emergency appointment. They told me to bring him in first thing the next morning (since the doctor was in surgery the day I called) and they would be sure to work us in. He was seen on day ten and it was confirmed that his foot had begun to die. The arteries had closed again and his foot would need to be amputated mid-tarsal (across the arch for us non-medical folks). Another angioplasty was scheduled and performed to re-open the arteries so the amputation would have the proper blood supply to heal. A few days later his foot was amputated in an outpatient surgical center. The procedure was without incident and we were sent home 30 minutes after he entered the recovery room. Everyone expected a full recovery.

At this time, it was well into July, Jason was a few weeks out of surgery and his pain was beginning to increase instead of fade. Back to the hospital we went. Despite our best efforts, the surgical site had begun to slowly die due to diminished blood flow. Every effort taken up to this point was aimed at saving his foot. Now we had to face the fact the only way to save his quality of life would be to sacrifice his leg for the greater good.

Looking back, I am amazed at how little we actually knew about the amputation process from surgery to recovery to life without a limb. August had just begun when Jason went from the hospital to in-patient rehab, to learn to be self-reliant when navigating stairs and shifting from standing to sitting and back.

This three month long medical crisis, in and of itself, was traumatic. While Jason was recovering from surgery and coming to terms with his new life, I was juggling more balls than I could count. I had two young boys at home to care for full time, a house to maintain, new housing to find, packing to do, and so much more. My days began early as I woke the boys and prepared them to spend the day with family. After driving them 33 miles each way to my mom's house, I would return home and spend an hour or two making phone calls to sort out which agencies might be able to help us with rent and utility bills. I was also looking for somewhere to move within our budget. Our income had been non-existent for 3 months now. We were surviving on state aid and family donations. These two hours a day were also dedicated to meeting with agencies and filling out paperwork. Afterward, I would head to the hospital or rehab center, crying all the tears I couldn't shed in front of the boys or Jason. Then I'd sit by Jason's side translating medical jargon and talking with doctors about the possibilities, probabilities, and options. At the end of visiting hours, I would kiss Jason goodbye and drive off into the sunset to pick up the boys before heading home, where I would prepare for another day of the same. It was an exhausting time, to say the least.

During this time, we were living in an apartment complex. It was nice and the apartment was spacious. But it all came at a price we could no longer afford. Because of my efforts and the generosity of others, we were able to stay current with our rent payments. But due to our lack of income, we were no longer qualified to renew our lease, which ended just a few weeks after Jason came home from rehab. It was nice to have him home, but the hours I had been spending driving to and from the rehab center were now dedicated to caring for an amputee which brought new challenges yet unimagined.

As it turns out, not many people are willing to take a risk on renting to a family with no income with a medically fragile member. So on September 1, 2016, we were officially homeless. It would take us three months and a Hail Mary save on my dad's part to secure housing. We moved in 10 days before Christmas. It was the best gift we could have received. During those three long months before this, we had graciously stayed with family while driving 200+ miles each way to doctor and specialist appointments. This was often four to five times a week. It tested our mettle but we made it through.

One month after moving into our new home, Jason was granted disability. He would soon begin receiving payments, roughly one-third of his previous earnings. However, it was steady and we were grateful.

One year after Jason's last amputation, his leg was healing (with a few minor and one major setback). He was being fitted with a prosthetic and our darkest days were behind us. The boys were in a new school and making friends. Jason's appointments reduced from four per week to five a month, and we found ourselves adjusting to a new "normal".

The three years between Jason's final amputation and this writing have been a series of ups and downs. We have welcomed each challenge and celebrated each success (usually with a well-deserved nap). The amputee life is definitely not for the faint of heart. The struggle is real and we hope that by sharing our story and the lessons learned that we can help other families celebrate the little victories and find peace in the storm.

Understanding Perspectives

When it starts as the amputation process and morphs into the amputation lifestyle, there are two different perspectives on the experience.

As the patient/amputee, your spouse will:

- be mourning the loss of their limb
- realizing they aren't immortal
- wondering how they will resume their previous lifestyle
- worrying about how they will be perceived by society
- and fretting over whether you will leave because s/he looks different and cannot do what s/he once did.

This is a lot of emotional and mental turmoil and they have nothing better to do than think about these things while lying in that hospital bed.

At the same time, you will be going through your own mental/emotional trauma.

You will find yourself worried about:

- the possibility of your spouse's death
- the household finances
- your children's welfare (if you have them)

- how financial obligations will be met
- growing hospital bills
- where the extra time will come from to accomplish everything
- and a myriad of daily living issues

At the same time, you will also find that your once loving spouse has become demanding/insulting/downright mean, that self-care and proper meals are non-existent, that your relationship has morphed from partners to caretaker/patient, and that date night has been replaced by long trips to appointments with doctors and specialists. It's almost more than a person can handle.

The biggest mistakes you could make at this time is believing that things will return to what they once were and that it's alright for him to unleash his anger and frustration on you because he is going through a lot. NO! I cannot say that loud enough. **It is never okay for him to unleash his anger and frustration on you.** It won't subside. Instead it will grow to epic proportions of mental and emotional abuse that will destroy you. They tend to take out most of their frustration on you, the caregiver but it isn't acceptable. If he is angry and frustrated, he needs to talk with a professional and get help. You have enough to deal with and don't need anyone making your life more difficult, including your spouse. They are not the only one going through this. Amputations affect the entire family.

As for returning to your previous life...you will find yourself mourning this loss for some time. Some days it will be easier than others, but at the end of the day, the life you once knew will be forever gone. Yes, your spouse will physically heal and (hopefully) mentally heal. There will be many things your spouse can resume doing which will ease your burden significantly. But this all takes some time and creativity. For instance, I struggle with mowing grass because I have a significant allergy to grasses. Even with his newest prosthetic, Jason cannot mow half an acre of grass with a self-propelled push mower. The strain on his residual limb causes pressure sores and physical exhaustion. So we remedied that by purchasing a second-hand riding lawn mower that he can operate even without his prosthetic on. Of course, there have been times when he ran out of gas and had to yell for help because he was stranded with no way to get back to the house except to crawl. Because standing for extended periods is difficult and painful he has also learned by trial and error how to change his cooking style from stove top to oven which allows him to sit while its cooking. There are many reasons that this creativity is important. It relieves you of some responsibilities but it also helps to rebuild his confidence and independence. Just because he can't do things the way he once did doesn't mean he can't do them at all. It just takes some out-of-the-box thinking.

Another important aspect of healing is to express what both of you are feeling. Sometimes couples need a neutral third party to mediate the exchange but this would depend on how strong your relationship was prior to amputation and the level of your communications skills. There will be times when you are angry at your spouse for allowing himself to be in a position that requires amputation. You will be frustrated by the extra burden that has been placed upon you. You will fret about the fact that he could have died. You will be so exhausted that you cannot think. And at times you will feel hopeless about your ability to get everything done. All the while he is getting attention from everyone because he lost a limb. You will often feel invisible and as if nobody sees you struggling. This can build up a wall of resentment that will need to be addressed or it will consume you and cause mass devastation.

From the spousal caretaker viewpoint, your spouse can come off as an overgrown demanding child. There will be days when you just want to tell him to get off his ass and make an effort to act like an adult. This is why communication is so important. Jason and I once discussed this in depth. I was exhausted from handling everything myself while all he did was sit in his chair watching TV and napping. The reality was that he didn't really HAVE an option. Many days he cannot wear his prosthetic for a variety of reasons. Other days he is immobilized with pain. He also has other medical conditions that directly affect his ability to participate in life. But to this tired and weary caregiver's mind: All that gets forgotten when I am dragging myself around to get everything done and he is 'just sitting there'. We still have these days. I'm not going to lie. But he makes more of an effort, especially on days when I tell him I am struggling. As it turns out, while I am wading hip deep through all these aforementioned feelings and thoughts, he is often buried in his own thoughts and sitting all day is more of a punishment than a luxury as he continues to mourn the loss of his freedom. As a new amputee, there is a lot of guilt. In one surgery they have shaken the very foundation of their life and the lives of their spouse and children. Concessions must be made. Priorities change. Finances may dry up. The workload shifts to be cruelly unfair. And there is nothing they can do to fix it. They get wrapped up in all the things they can no longer do...climbing the ladder to clean the gutters, picking a crying kid up off the floor, being independent, etc. The list never really ends. It becomes an ever-playing loop in their mind while your mind becomes so weary that you cannot think of anything.

Stepping up to the Challenge

When everything goes sideways and change seems to affect every aspect of your life, it can feel like there is little positive in all the negative. Even the smallest positive is something to hold on to though. Remember that.

On bad days it helps to focus on a few positives. On particularly stressful days write down on a scrap of paper three things you're grateful for. As you find yourself greeted by a new stressor, simply re-read your list as a reminder that there is still good happening in your life.

I am _____.

I can _____ really well.

Life is _____.

Today I am grateful for:

                      1.

                      2.

                      3.

When Jason lost his leg it only touched the surface of our losses. In a three-month time span we lost our income, our apartment, many of our friends, most of our future plans, and our ability to properly provide for our children. When the dust settled, we looked around to find ourselves at rock bottom. With the exception of our lives, there was little left for us to lose. Everyone's rock bottom looks different. The funny thing about being on rock bottom is that while the fall is terrifying and the landing is painful, being on rock bottom holds hope beyond all hope. You fell, you landed, and most importantly...you survived. There is only one direction to go from rock bottom and that is up. This is a time to think big, make plans, and get to work creating something better than before.

Of course, you're also physically tired, emotionally exhausted, unsure which way really is up, and you're busy mopping up the mess, while not realizing you haven't shut off the water. The key point to take away is that this is an opportunity to change your life for the better (whatever that means to you and your family). Maybe it is an opportunity for your spouse to spend more time with your kids. Maybe it is time to go back to school. Maybe you'll find yourself moving into a new home (hopefully one that is affordable and wheelchair accessible).

When we found ourselves at rock bottom, we saw it as the opportunity that it was. We had a blank slate and could become anything we desired. We were homeless, so we could choose our housing style and location. We were jobless, so we had the options of getting trained in something new, working with our current training, working for minimum wage, or working for ourselves. Of course, in reality, the sky isn't the limit. The actual limits are set by your income, your creativity and your determination.

In the end we decided to begin at the end. We looked hard at what our dream life would look like. This time we devoted ourselves to the details. Due to Jason's multiple health problems he was granted disability. It was significantly less than we were used to living on, but if we were dedicated, we could meet our needs and remain debt-free. We ditched our credit card and figured out a workable budget. With our basic needs met, we returned to the drawing board. The housing my dad had secured for us was "up north", so we had met that goal. While I had hoped to be further up north, the community we are in is great for our children and allows us to get to medical care easily. We have decided to stay in this community and are now focused on what we want in the house we will one day purchase.

Prior to landing at rock bottom, I had enjoyed the freedom of renting a home. It allowed us to move around to various communities and freed up funds that would have otherwise gone to repairs and maintenance. After rock bottom, we were both more interested in the security of home ownership (though to be honest I would love to just own a travel trailer and live the nomadic life). Jason has also changed his desire to have a large house. He has realized the difficulty of maintaining such a large space as well as the logistics of navigating so much space to meet basic needs. He has now narrowed his dream to a single story home of approximately 400 to 500 square feet. With these details nailed down we started working on location, property features, and how to finance it all. However, in full disclosure, we are currently have exactly zero dollars saved to buy a house. The amputee life isn't a fairy tale, but having goals and dreams helps make the days a little brighter.

If, like us, you find yourself sitting at rock bottom, glance up at the stars above, dream, pray, and take this chance to plan a future that will fulfill of all your greatest desires.

The amputee path\lifestyle isn't for the faint of heart. It challenges you in ways you never would have imagined. Hospitals and doctor offices become second homes, vacations get pushed aside for appointments with specialists. Your time becomes more valuable than ever before. Maybe you are lucky enough to live in the same town as your hospital (we have to travel over an hour to ours). If you must travel for hospitalizations, one suggestion I have during extended hospital stays is to take advantage of your RV or ask to borrow one from a friend or family member. While there is nothing quite as wonderful as sleeping in your own bed, there is something to be said about not having to spend hours on the road each day commuting. Many hospitals have ample parking and will allow you to dry dock an RV in the back lots where few people park. This is one luxury I wished to have so many times and I am currently working on investing in a small RV for this reason. Some hospitals allow spouses to stay in the patient's room. Our hospital does because every room is private. There are certain floors that do prohibit overnight guests due to logistics though, such as ICU and the heart floor. Other hospitals prohibit overnight stays across the board because they have shared rooms. You can ask what your hospital's policy is. I do recommend the RV idea though because it means that you can enjoy uninterrupted sleep. It is amazing how frequently hospital staff walk into a hospital room throughout the night and how little rest is actually achievable.

Another challenge you will face is time constraints and the pull between your children, your hospitalized spouse, your household responsibilities, and your job. You are not a comic book super hero. There are limits to your abilities to operate without sleep, food, and showers. When it comes to your children, especially if they have not reached their teen years yet, try to prioritize them. While it will be necessary to shuttle them off to family or friends from time to time while you are at work or the hospital, it is important to keep their routine as normal as possible. Trust me, this will cut back on tantrums, hurt or angry feelings, and trauma. Maybe you need to have Aunt Linda take your son to karate this week, but it is better than having him miss class because you are too exhausted to take him or there just weren't enough hours in the day. We often think that most of the time children are oblivious to the cares of the world. But during these stressful hospitalizations, you must remember that your children know that their parent is in the hospital and will be coming out changed. They may not know the details but they do feel the stress and keeping their daily routines intact will help a lot.

The next priority is your job. This is the main pillar preventing your lives from total collapse and this income may be the only one you have. With that being said, nobody has ever laid on their deathbed and exclaimed "I wish I had spent more time at work." If you work for a public agency, a private or public K-12 school or college, or for a company that employs over 50 people, you are eligible to take advantage of the Family Medical Leave Act. This is an act "designed to help employees balance their work and family responsibilities by allowing them to take reasonable UNPAID leave for certain family and medical reasons." While you won't receive your usual pay, this act does protect your job (and continues your insurance through your employer) while you "care for an immediate family member (i.e. spouse, child, or parent) with a serious health condition", among other things. To qualify you need to have worked for your current employer for "at least 12 months, at least 1,250 hours over the past 12 months, and work at a location where the company employs 50 or more employees within 75 miles." This will provide you with 12 weeks of protected leave. There may be subtle differences from state to state, so do a little research. It is quite a relief to know that you can take time off to care for your spouse without jeopardizing your career.

We are now down to your hospitalized spouse and housework. In any situation you never fail by choosing the human factor. Housework will always be there. Trust me, it's ALWAYS waiting. So as long as your children (and yourself) are not running around naked due to a lack of clean clothes, don't waste much of your precious time on housework. As my friend, Jeanne, says "Your tombstone will never read: 'She had the cleanest home in town!'" It is even ok to pick up a pack of paper plates and paper cups to get you through.

Now, let's discuss your spouse. If you are new to the amputee life you will find yourself wrapped up in your spouse's medical adventure. Every decision you make will be weighed against being by his side and easing his pain/worry. And for the most part it should be. That's what we do. We rush to the bedside of those with medical issues. Deep down we want to help. We want them to know they aren't alone. We soothe our own fears of facing such a life changing situation alone by preventing someone else from going it alone. All the while hoping: if the situation ever arises, that someone will be there for us as well.

During Jason's hospitalization for his second amputation, our children were on summer break so they spent their days at their grandma's house while I was visiting their dad in the hospital. They came home in the evenings with me, and enjoyed eating a good meal and swimming or going for a walk or whatnot. During Jason's initial hospitalization, my days were long. They began at 6:30am and sometimes didn't end until well after 11pm. In these three years I have pushed aside my need for sleep and self-care because "Jason and the boys needed me" much to my own demise. Over time it will get easier to determine the moments that need your sacrifice and those that can handle themselves. After all, the saying goes... *if you don't make time for your wellness, you'll be forced to make time for your illness*. One time recently I had driven my children to my mom's house early in the morning so I could sit with Jason all day. Around dinner time I left to drive the 30 miles to pick them up and then the 52 miles home from my mom's house. As I found our exit off the highway I was feeling relief that I would soon have food in my belly and a comfy bed under my weary body. Then my phone rang. Jason was on the other end. He had become severely anemic and they were prepping him for a blood transfusion. He was out of his mind with worry and wanted me to come back so he didn't have to face this alone. (When all was said and done, he would need three bags of blood to become stable again.) So much for a meal and a bed. I called my mom and asked if she could take the boys overnight. We ate fast food that night as I drove another 52 miles to drop them off. Then I continued on for the extra 30 miles to the hospital. I arrived just minutes after the first bag of blood was hooked up and tried to sleep in the world's most uncomfortable excuse for a recliner. But he wasn't alone so that was all that mattered.

These highly charged life altering situations happen. They happen out of nowhere and they happen more than you could ever imagine. But here is what I have learned in the last three years...

1. Your spouse has a care team at his disposal in the hospital.

2. There are other family members and friends who can sit with your spouse to keep him company in between tests and when he is bored

3. You are only one person. You may be a great person, a caring person, a strong person...but you are still only one person. And when you burn out? Then what?

These three points are truly going to make or break you. While it will be important for you to be an advocate for your spouse and to assist him with understanding procedures, test results, and such, there is nothing you can medically do for him. Your presence is not needed at his bedside 24/7. No matter how much he insists you need to be there. Unless you really enjoy emptying urinals and assisting with bathroom trips and running for water and doing a myriad of other tasks he would prefer you to do than the paid staff. Of course you should make every attempt to be there for procedures, test results, surgeries and such but just because he is bored with tv and wants someone to talk to, doesn't mean it has to be you. Call friends and family and set up times for them to visit your spouse throughout the hospital stay. Or better yet, tell your spouse to call them personally.

If you don't listen to the advice of numbers one and two above, please read number three until it fully sinks in. When you are trying to decide where your time will be spent and what needs to be done. You must remember that you need to include yourself on that list. So many times I would wake up in a fog of exhaustion only to realize I couldn't actually remember my last shower or hot meal or whether I intentionally put my hair in a bun or if it was just so matted from a lack of brushing that it became a tangled mess. Your spouse has a care team and later on I will show you how to create one for yourself.

Helping your spouse through the amputee process is definitely a challenge. And because you love your spouse you will step up to that challenge without hesitation. In the beginning this will all seem like a 100-yard dash but it is important for you to know (and I wish I had known) that this is really more of a marathon. Pace yourself, seek support, and don't forget to slow down from time to time to get a drink of water.

From Partner to Caregiver

When you are a spouse, you can count on your significant other to show affection when you need it, to listen when you're scared or frustrated, to hold you when you cry, to pick up the slack when your load is too heavy, and to assist in problem solving. And you most likely do the same for him/her.

Becoming a spousal caregiver changes that dynamic. For some couples this can be a temporary situation, for others it can become permanent. It really depends on the foundation of your relationship pre-amputation and how your spouse is able to function afterward. This transition from spouse to Caregiver isn't a slippery slope that you plummet down at warp speed and land at the bottom with a thud. Instead it is more like an escalator...you're going about your business, doing what needs to be done. You may notice small changes. But when you get to the bottom you realize that everything has changed and you can't pinpoint a specific time when it happened.

We become spousal caretakers when our significant other battles a long-term health event. What had begun as "in sickness and in health" has now leveled up to a new dimension of love, frustration, and commitment that you never imagined possible. You're happy to assist your spouse with getting in the shower or to bring him a urinal when he physically cannot make it to the bathroom. It seems natural that you would drive him to doctor appointments and spend countless nights sleeping in a hospital chair next to his bed so he doesn't have to be alone. It doesn't even cross your mind to seek out direct care workers for help with care tasks. The emotional exhaustion you feel is at constant odds with the guilt of being healthy and not getting everything done. This is what love looks like, right? It is all about stepping up to the battle, fully prepared to fight the good fight. It is believing in a quick resolution/recovery and hoping for a brighter future.

During our marriage we have won many medical battles yet we still find ourselves amidst the war. I am still as steadfast as ever to see this war through to the end but I am tired. Oh so very tired. And there are days when I wish I could sit out a battle or two.

Having a medical emergency or chronic medical issue is frightening for the patient. They focus on what it all means in terms of life span, quality of life, pain endurance, etc. They find themselves facing their greatest demons head-on. They're so consumed that they fail to see the toll their health takes on you as the healthy spouse. Or at least this is what I once believed. As it turns out, they do realize the toll it takes on their spouse. They see us struggle to do things they once did for the family and they carry guilt over the burden they perceive themselves to be on us as well.

Last year I began journaling as a way to clear my head and tap into a calm place where I could rest and regroup. It was journaling that helped me to see how our relationship had changed. Before that I had been so busy that it never occurred to me all the changes we had undergone. We no longer held hands or hugged because the physical contact of such acts contributed to the chronic pain he endures. I stopped relying on him for comfort and support because I knew he was already beating himself up over the situation we were in and his inability to change it. So many hours were spent drying his tears as he faced countless surgeries, tests, procedures, and unanswered questions that I became skilled at holding mine back until they consumed me.

After being released from the hospital I thought maybe everything would go back to normal. The truth is that this became our new normal. We began sleeping in separate beds because he now struggled with sleep and I was in desperate need of it. Not to mention he had become overly protective of his stump to the point of paranoia about being kicked or injured.

Our lunch dates were replaced with long unromantic drives to doctor appointments. In the blink of an eye everything we believed represented love was stripped away leaving us wondering what was left. As it turned out, we sleep better separately. The main reason we slept in the same bed was because that's what married couples do. The reality was that we were never happy because I need a soft mattress and he loves a firm mattress. And then there is the blanket situation. We always had our own bedding. He preferred a single blanket whereas I need to be buried under 87 pounds of blankets. Those long drives to and from appointments were also a blessing. Our marriage had suffered greatly over the years due to a lack of communication. He was always working and we rarely spent any time together. The long drives gave us one-on-one time to talk about everything and anything. To be honest, I think I have gotten to know him better in these past three years than I had in the previous twelve.

Looking back, I can see the unfolding of our relationship but I am not going to lie and tell you it was a smooth transition. It was by far the scariest, ugliest, and most difficult time in my life. As selfish and yet obvious as it sounds, you must learn to depend on yourself and to take care of yourself. Your spouse cannot be responsible for your self-worth, happiness, or feeling loved. You must learn to take care of your own needs. As a spousal caregiver it's easy to become so focused on your loved one's needs that you forget that you have needs of your own. It is proper to help your spouse when they need it but you must also help yourself. As the saying goes, *'You cannot pour from an empty cup'*. If you think doing it all is difficult when well, try doing it while battling a head cold or the flu. Or having sick kids AND a needy spouse. Sheesh!

It is of utmost importance that if you find yourself caring for your spouse as they go through a medical emergency, even if it is a short term event, that you do some specific things immediately. There is no particular order to complete these. Your life will run a bit smoother if you do them.

1. Make sure you know your spouse's medical and final wishes. They may not be in imminent danger of death or unconsciousness but it is better to know:

    - whether they want to be on life support
    - if they believe in transfusions
    - and their views on organ donation

It is better to know this information and not need to use the it than it is to need the information and have to guess.

2. Check into your state's laws to make sure you have a legal right to make medical decisions on your spouse's behalf. Some states give spouses more rights than others. If your state doesn't grant spouses the power to make medical choices on the patient's behalf, make sure you have your spouse fill out a durable power of attorney form that grants you the power to make their decisions if they can't do it themselves.

3. Find/create your support team early on. In the beginning you will be refreshed and up for the challenges, blissfully unaware of how long this race really is. By the time you realize you're

sinking, it is a bit late to start building a boat. At the very least, have a list of potential support people that you can start recruiting as needs arise.

4. Create a journal and write in it. Record your spouse's medical journey, your feelings, your fears, the names of everyone who has helped you and your family, the frustrations of your journey, and the milestones reached. Who knows, one day it could be a best seller. At the least, it can get that all out of your head to allow you space to think. And remember that this journal is just for you. It doesn't require proper sentences, punctuation, straight lines, or even words. You can scribble, draw, or tear pages out just to watch them burn.

5. Pack "go" bags in the beginning. I have included packing lists for each bag. If they are created early on and repacked after each use they will always be ready. When the next medical emergency hits you will be more prepared and comfortable. These days we are constantly hearing about 72-hour go bags. They are the must-have of the prepper world. But they can also be a godsend to amputees and their families. Since your purpose is to survive a hospitalization your packing list will be a bit different than that of a prepper go bag. But the idea is the same...to have a bag ready with the essentials when you need them. My

husband needs desperately to believe that he won't ever have to go back to the hospital so I keep our bags in a closet where they are out of sight but accessible. Below I have made easy packing lists. There is one for your amputee spouse, another for yourself, and a third list for when you have to bring children along. Feel free to consider these lists to be a guide. Add any other items you feel are necessary. If possible, buy seconds of items you use daily such as toothpaste and phone chargers so you don't have to pack these items while trying to get to the hospital. Ideally you should only have to grab your phone, purse/wallet, and the go bags.

6. During your spouse's extended hospital stays, be sure to make your bed every morning. I know I sound like a 1950's mom but there is a loving logic behind it. During medical emergencies floors will go un-swept, laundry will go unwashed, and dishes may pile up. But there is something divinely soothing to be able to walk away from the hospital, through the messy house and fall into the beautifully made safe haven of your bed. It is like a loving welcome home hug.

7. When loved ones ask what they can do to help, take this question seriously. Don't brush their offer off with pat responses like "nothing" or "pray for us". They want to help but may not know what you actually need. Ask them to wash a

load of laundry, put away the clean dishes, sweep the floor, bring you a cheeseburger, braid your hair, etc. Just make sure the request is something they are willing and able to do. Many hands make for lighter work. That cheeseburger may have cost them $2 and a 15-minute drive to the restaurant (or maybe they made it themselves) but it could be the only thing you have eaten all day as you impatiently wait for your spouse to come out of a surgery that should've been completed 1 hour and 47 minutes ago and nobody has said anything to you about the delay. The key to making these requests is to properly thank the person doing them and tell them specifically the difference they have made. Cleaning a load of laundry isn't glamorous and seems like an insignificant task but it takes on a different meaning for the person completing it when it is followed by "thank you so much for washing and drying those clothes! It is one less thing that I have to do now and I can feel better about sending the kids out in public."

8. Use the hospital's chapel. It is open to every person of every belief system. It is also rarely used. I admit that I frequently passed it by without a second glance more times than I can count. It always seemed to be for people pleading with their higher power to spare the life of whatever loved one they were visiting. The truth

is that the chapel can be a great refuge during your spouse's extended hospital stays. When they are sleeping off anesthesia or have been taken for a test or procedure there is no reason you must sit in their hospital room which is often way too cold or hot to be comfortable, surrounded by the harsh lights and the jarring noises of machines, other patients and hospital staff. Use this time to escape it all. Make your way down to the chapel and indulge your senses in the quietness, soft lighting, and comfortable seating found there. This is a safe space where nothing is expected of you. Nobody is demanding anything of you. Nothing has to be accomplished. Just be. Read a book. Cry your eyes out. Say a prayer. Take a nap. Whatever comes into your mind and soothes your heart.

9. Plan a welcome home celebration for the day your spouse is going to be released. This isn't a party. It will be just you, him, and your kids (if you have them). Make a simple banner (or purchase one) that says 'welcome home' and hang it in front of wherever your spouse will be (on the wall in front of his easy chair, across from his bed, etc). Have comfy pillows and blankets ready. Decide on a good meal. And choose a favorite movie or television show to share together. Maybe even throw in a dessert. Neither of you will be up for a night on the town but the two of you just made it

over a giant hurdle and deserve to celebrate your victory even if only in the smallest of ways.

10. Write thank you notes to everyone who has helped you. It doesn't matter if you've already said thank you. It doesn't matter if it is their job to help you. And it doesn't matter if it cost them nothing to help. Send out a thank you card. People don't get real mail anymore. It is usually bills and advertisements. Receiving a thank you card means a lot. You don't have to write pages, just a simple sentence inside explaining how appreciative you are for their generosity will suffice. Let the nurses on whatever floor he was on see that they made a difference. That state aid worker who got you emergency help because what started out as a request for help quickly escalated into a full blown nervous breakdown gets a thank you card. That receptionist who copied your spouse's file and waived the fee because she knew you were struggling deserves a card. Your Aunt Penny gets a card for that time she brought over a sweater to the hospital because you were freezing. No act should go unacknowledged. Trust me, the recipients will be more endeared to helping you again in the future and there will definitely be a future need for help.

As I said earlier, I have set out to write the guide I wish I had had during our initial medical emergency. The insights and advice presented throughout this book have been obtained through trial and error and over years of experience. I hope that you find this book to be a valuable resource and refer to it often for inspiration and ideas.

Bag for Amputee Spouse

- 2 pairs underwear
- 2 pajama sets
- Eyeglasses/contact lenses and cases/solution
- Denture case and cleanser
- Toothbrush/toothpaste
- Hairbrush/comb
- Hair tie
- Deodorant
- Sanitary products
- Book/magazine/tablet (with charger)
- Family photo
- Medical log
- Cell phone charger
- Prosthetic and all paraphernalia needed to use it

Bag for Yourself

- Full change of clothes
- Comfortable shoes/slippers
- Toothbrush/toothpaste
- Hairbrush
- Hair tie
- Contact lenses/ eyeglass case/ contact solution
- Books/magazines/tablet (and charger)
- Cellphone charger
- Family phone numbers
- Cash
- Bottles of water or a water bottle
- High protein snacks
- Lap blanket
- Long sleeve shirt
- Medications (yours, not theirs)
- Medical dictionary
- This guide

<u>Bag for children</u>

- Long sleeve shirt
- Pajamas
- Small blanket
- Quiet toys that do not roll
- Bottles of water
- Low-mess snacks
- Travel size board games
- appropriate books
- Socks
- Wipes
- A diaper bag (if you have an infant or toddler)

The Anatomy of your Support Team

Your spouse will naturally develop a support/medical team as s/he navigates the path into the amputee world. They will have doctors and specialists crawling out of the woodwork. Friends and family will ask frequently about their well-being. This will happen almost to the exclusion of your existence. It is a statement that is often iterated by amputee spouses, "Why doesn't anyone ever ask how I am doing?" As the spouse of an amputee you will need a support group for yourself. This will require some deep thinking and outreach on your part but it will be both necessary and helpful.

Before we get too deep into this, let's look at what a support team is and what yours will look like. A support team is a group of individuals brought together for a specific purpose. Each member will embody a specific set of skills and knowledge that contributes to the success of the overall purpose of the group. In the business world these people tend to be professionals with specific training, education, or experience. In the spousal caregiver world this team will be made up of individuals with specific experiences, personal connections, and diverse personality traits/hobbies. Some members of your team will be familiar with your situation (such as family and friends) while others will be members of the community that you specifically seek out (counselors, therapists, online and in-person support groups).

In today's world people seem to be busier than ever. Those who love you will want to help you in your time of need but will most likely have no idea of what it is you really need. They may also be secretly concerned with the time commitment of offering help. You will also find that help fades with time. People will come out of the woodwork during the initial phases as your spouse is becoming an amputee. Yet few will notice the struggle you will experience once he is home and again during subsequent hospitalizations (and trust me, there will be many). By being specific in your requests you will most likely get your needs met and allow your loved ones to ease your burden in meaningful ways.

Your support team will consist of three separate categories of people though some people may fall into more than one category. The key is to ask enough of, but not too much, of any one person on your team and always keep their strengths in mind when choosing what to ask of each individual. For instance, you wouldn't ask Aunt Bernadette with the fear of dogs to watch your pooch so you can be at the hospital.

The first category I will begin with is Spirituality. I begin with this category because it is pretty easy to find individuals to join this team. These people often share your spiritual beliefs and upon hearing of your dilemma they will offer to pray for your family, add you to a prayer chain, and make sure you have rides to church. Even if people are of a different faith they will often pull together to raise you and your family in blessings of their faith.

Our family happens to follow a pagan path. We deeply believe in the value and interconnectedness of all life. During the initial three months of our amputation journey, many Christian family members and friends offered to pray for our safe travels through our trials. When I would go to agencies and organizations for assistance with a bill or with food, they would almost always ask if they could pray with me. My answer was always yes. It didn't matter that we had different ideologies, what mattered in that moment was that another human soul was willing to stand up next to my fallen family and send intentions (prayers) out into the universe on our behalf. It is a small but powerful act as it serves as a reminder that even strangers are rooting for your family to win.

The second category of your support team will be those individuals that prioritize your mental and emotional needs. These people are more vested in your life such as a close friend, a sibling, or a parent. This group can (and probably should) also include counselors, therapists, and mental health call centers. It is a good idea to have a solid mix of both professionals and loved ones on your team. Most importantly, seek out a support group for caregivers of amputees, even if it is only online. From experience I have learned that the trials and tribulations of amputees and their spouses are often incomprehensible to those who have never been on the amputee path. It is akin to being the only French speaking person in a room full of Spaniards. There are vast differences in experience, frustrations, terminology, priorities, etc.

When your spouse suffers through a long-term medical trauma, you will find yourself meandering back and forth through the seven stages of grief even though you are not the one in the hospital bed. Some stages will be more disturbing than others. For example, when my husband lost his leg there was no direct risk to his life. For all intents and purposes, he was fully expected to, one day, leave the hospital and resume his life. This didn't stop the late night thoughts we both found ourselves plagued with regarding the possibility of his premature death and what it would mean to our family. The key is to acknowledge your feelings in each stage, without judgement, and process it to allow for growth to happen. It is also important to remember that you and your spouse will travel through different stages of grief at different times and stay in stages for different amounts of time. **If ever you find yourself struggling with a particular stage, seek professional help. Do not fall into the all-to-common trap of "s/he's the one in the medical crisis. I should be happy with my health." You don't have to be physically injured to get help. Needing help is black and white. Either you need help with a mental/physical/spiritual issue or you don't. There is no gradation or room for**

comparison. Your need does not need to be worse than what your spouse is enduring for you to be worthy of help just as your needs do not become trivial because they are not as significant as your spouse's needs. If you breathe air and have feelings, you are valid and have a right to do what is needed to help you be your best.

With that said, let's look at the seven stages of grief. The first stage is shock and disbelief. At first this will be overwhelming, but it will become a strange normal after a while, kind of like a morbid game of peek-a-boo. You will know it is hiding somewhere but will jump a little every time it jumps out at you. For ease of informing, the seven stages are often listed as a linear path.

- Shock/Disbelief is followed by
- Denial which leads to Guilt,
- then Bargaining,
- Depression, Loneliness,
- Reflection,
- Reconstruction/Working Through,
- and finally Acceptance.

In real life the stages of grief look less like a clear path and more like a corn maze. The amount of time a person stays in any one stage fluctuates greatly as sometimes you will seem to progress nicely through the maze, other times you will need to back track to make progress, and sometimes you will find yourself sitting in a dead end, head in hands, bawling your eyes out because the only solution you can come up with is to eat your way out of the maze.

What I found most intriguing and disturbing was the range of emotions within a stage. There were times I was in denial about our circumstances while at other times I completely denied the reality of how our lives would be forever changed. Many times my guilt would swing from guilt over my fear of Jason dying (though he wasn't in imminent danger) to guilt about not having pushed him more to seek medical intervention sooner. This was followed by disbelief that I had not foreseen that this would all happen and my lack of preparation for what was to come. There were many times I found myself frustrated at how difficult it was to find help. I was angry at myself for not being able to function without sleep. I was equally angry at Jason for allowing this all to happen to us (even though he didn't will his body to create massive blood clots). Then there was my frustration at myself for not being able to fix everything instantly.

During the stages of grief, you will most likely encounter darker thoughts than you want to admit to yourself, much less to your friends and family. These won't necessarily be thoughts of self-harm or murder but there will be moments where the stress is so great you may have thoughts of how life would be better without your spouse. There may also be angry thoughts of how you are paying for the consequences of your spouse's poor choices (even if his/her amputation was not actually caused by their choices). These types of thoughts are easier to share with trained professionals because there isn't the stigma of judgment attached. These professionals will also be the best prepared to help you work through your current circumstances and the emotional waves those circumstances have caused.

The other members of your care team for mental/emotional needs will most likely be close friends and family. While you may be accustomed to your spouse filling that role, you will soon realize that they aren't as emotionally available as you'd like them to be at this time. And trust me, this won't change once they leave the hospital. From personal experience and talking with other amputee spouses, it takes quite a bit of work getting them to notice that other people exist.

Another thing you may notice is that while family and friends may want to be there to support your mental and emotional needs, they may not exactly know what your needs are and how to meet them. Unless you've experienced these unique circumstances you really cannot fathom the extent of emotional trauma the caregiver spouse truly endures. In fact, as you are going through the trauma you may not even know what it is that you need. For this reason, I am presenting you with a list of actions that your loved one can do to support you mentally/emotionally.

- A one-minute hug (actually set a timer for this. You will be amazed at how long one minute actually is)
- Have them write down a few words of encouragement on a scrap of paper. Think of fortune cookie fortunes...short and simple. Just something you can carry in your pocket and peek at from time to time.
- Spend the night with you. Sleep is often sketchy when we are worried out of our minds. Having a best friend, mom, or sibling stay over for a night could help you rest. Especially when you're accustomed to not sleeping alone.
- Meet up to plan an escape or welcome home party or dream vacation. Plan out all the details. Money is no object. Add photos if you can. Who will be there? What will the décor look like? Where will this event happen? What do you need to pack? How will you invite people? You most likely will not follow through on these plans for a myriad of reasons but it's a great mental break and a good reminder that happiness can still happen.
- Ask them to prepare your favorite meal and/or dessert for you. Even if your lack of appetite prevents you from eating more than

a bite or two, the love you feel will nourish you.

- Ask them to call and check on you at specific times such as after important test results come in or during your spouse's surgery or any other time you have just come through something potentially life changing.
- Ask them to contact a specific agency on your behalf to get whatever information you need from them. Many agencies have rules in place that require personalized information can only be shared with those on the account. Often the recipient must apply in person to receive benefits, but that doesn't mean that a loved one can't ease your mental burden by doing a little legwork to get answers to general questions. They can also locate the proper person you need to talk to and obtain a list of paperwork/proofs you need to bring when filling out applications or attending appointments.
- Have them tell you the story of how you met or of their favorite memory of the two of you together. The funnier the better.
- Have them reach out to your spouse's family and friends on your behalf to schedule hospital visits to free up time for you to take a break.

- Watch a movie together with snacks and comfy blankets and such.

These are some things I needed and asked for. You can use these ideas or maybe you have a few of your own that are coming to mind. Whatever will help you most is good.

The third area of support is your physical needs. This is by far the easiest area to create a list from considering that we always have to-do lists waiting to be completed. The problem is that the items on your to-do list don't magically disappear when a spouse is hospitalized. In many instances, it actually grows longer. We know that everyone has a to-do list but it isn't obvious to most that doing something as mundane as sweeping the floor or walking the dog could really help a family during a medical crisis. The following is a list of items you can ask friends and family to help with. Remember though that they also have responsibilities so you should just choose one item that would make a big impact for you. Make sure that it is something they are capable of doing and possibly enjoy doing.

- Vacuum the living room
- Wash the dishes
- One hour of free childcare
- Walk the dog
- Feed the animals

- Drive you to the hospital (and maybe even pick you back up)
- Prepare a meal
- Watch your children while you shower
- Water the plants
- Go for a walk with you
- Return your library books
- Make the beds
- Mend clothes
- Wash a load of laundry
- Pick up basic groceries
- Pick up your prescriptions
- Clean out old food from refrigerator
- Change cat litter
- Fill up your gas tank (with money you provide, of course)

When your spouse undergoes a medical emergency or long-term medical event, everyone will be curious about the details. This can be exhausting, both physically and mentally, as you recount the drama for each individual. While it would be helpful to have others around to offer assistance with basic household tasks, there will be times when you just don't have it in you to entertain anyone. When people visit, we often feel obligated to give them undivided attention. It is important to know your limits and it is acceptable to simply tell people that you are not capable of having visitors at this time. Do not do anything that is beyond your current mental/physical/financial abilities during your spouse's hospitalizations. Remember, self-care is imperative. A friend of mine also pointed out that it would be beneficial to dedicate your Facebook page (or create a specific one) to providing updates on your spouse. This way, you can post quick updates and when others start asking about the situation, you can simply direct them to the page while avoiding lengthy rehashing.

If you have children or pets that you will be asking for help with, the following lists may be helpful to have filled out ahead of time. They can be left with whomever is caring for your pets or children and will offer you a little more peace of mind.

Childcare Instructions

(fill out one per child and update annually)

- Child's full name:
- Birthday:
- Immunizations:
- Allergies:
- Previous surgeries:
- Favorite book(s):
- Favorite food(s):
- Favorite snack(s):
- Naptime:
- Naptime routine:
- Bedtime:
- Bedtime routine:
- Waking time (morning and after naps):
- Wake up routine(s):
- Your contact information:
- Emergency contact (list at least two):
- Siblings:
- Child's doctor and their contact info:
- Preferred hospital for treatment:

Pet Care Instructions

(again, fill out a separate form for each pet):

- Pet name:
- Type of pet:
- Breed:
- Age and sex:
- Neutered/spayed: Yes. No.
- Updated shots: Yes. No.
- Feeding times:
- Food location:
- Serving size:
- Special feeding instructions:
- Toileting supply location:
- Special ticketing instructions:
- Special needs:
- Restricted home areas:
- Veterinarian name and contact information:
- Kennel information:
- Name and contact information of someone familiar with this pet that could help if needed:

Taking Care of the Care Taker

"Self-care" is a term we hear thrown around a lot lately. Depending on who you talk to, self-care can range from something as simple as brushing your hair to something as extravagant as spending a day at a full-service spa. When our spouse becomes an amputee we find our priorities shift and demands on our time increase. For our purposes we will loosely define 'self-care' as any act of kindness directed towards yourself for the sole purpose of rejuvenating your mind/body/spirit. You should aim to do three self-care activities a day. If you're busy, you should do five. Feel free to pick and choose the ideas that resonate with you and by all means, feel free to add your own ideas.

- Read a book
- Watch your favorite TV show
- Meditate
- Workout
- Eat a meal by candlelight
- Listen to good music
- Take a hot bubble bath
- Color a picture
- Paint
- Take a nap
- Read yourself a bedtime story
- Have dessert

- Plan a dream vacation with no regard to money
- Visit a garden
- Take a walk in nature
- Go swimming
- Build a snowman
- Create a vision board
- Write in a journal
- Play a game
- Jump rope
- Call a friend
- Wash laundry
- Make your bed
- Enjoy a cup of hot tea or coffee
- Wrap up in a cozy blanket
- Grow a plant
- Spend 24 hours away from social media
- Get a haircut
- Go for a bike ride
- Build a blanket fort
- Blow bubbles
- Work on a craft
- Treat yourself
- Camp in your backyard
- Observe the moon and stars
- Press flowers or leaves
- One-minute hug
- Enjoy lemonade in the sunshine

- Walk in the woods
- Look at vacation or family photos
- Indulge in your favorite chocolate treat
- Visit a park
- Sing a song
- Dance in the rain
- Play hopscotch
- Sleep for eight hours in a row
- Brush your hair
- Write yourself a letter expressing how much you appreciate all you do
- Play with a pet
- Say no to something you don't want to do
- Say yes to a new adventure
- Drink enough water
- Eat enough fruits and veggies
- Have a picnic for yourself
- Write in a journal

Because you are emotionally invested in your spouse and the outcome of their medical emergency will directly impact your life, you may feel obligated to surrender yourself to the greater cause. When you put your own care first, you may feel selfish or guilty but you shouldn't. Doctors and nurses spend their days caring for others. Yes, they get paid for it but what you should take from their example is that at the end of their shift they go home and take care of themselves. They rest, eat, shower, and do whatever is required to maintain their health and happiness. You should be doing the same. There is no law that requires you to sacrifice yourself on the altar of love and dedicate every moment to caring for your spouse.

In this time of chaos and uncertainty, it will be ever more imperative that you rest, perform necessary personal care, and assure that you are meeting all of your emotional, physical, spiritual, and mental needs. There are people who will assist you with this if you seek them out but ultimately the only one who can do this is you.

If you are reading this and thinking 'when could I possibly have time for self-care?!', you might not be aware of how much time we waste on any given day. Between the television, social media, email, and electronic games, we can easily lose hours before we even know what has happened. The biggest time waster though is worry. Often we worry about things that could possibly happen but never actually come to fruition. While we may multitask while worrying, we still rob ourselves of the mental energy that worry requires. One of the most helpful tools I have found to combat excessive worry during hospitalizations is to write them down. You've probably heard people talking about their bucket lists. All those places they want to see, the items they want to own, and the people they want to meet. Well, I present to you my Chuck-it List. When I found myself worrying about how a test can come out, or about a procedure or what it means if Jason dies, how I would take care of him if he got worse, etc. I would get so overwhelmed that I was completely useless. While we were homeless I was so bogged down in worries that I am surprised I was able to breathe. Taking care of a recently released amputee and two children while living out of suitcases and sleeping on a living room floor was where I found my breaking point. One day I came up with the Chuck-it list. It is simply another list to add to my many lists. But what makes this one special is that it is full of everything I am worried about. (This comes in especially handy at night when you can't shut your mind off). Simply write down everything on your mind...worries, things you need to do, questions you need to ask, etc. put it all on there. Then you will be able to relax a bit more because you know that you won't be forgetting anything. The next day read over the list. If it is an item that should actually be on your to-do list, move it there. If it is a worry about something that may or may not happen, leave it on the chuck-it list. When your chuck-it list is full, crumple it up then go outside and bury it in the ground. If you happen to live in the north and the ground is frozen, toss it in a fire. Just be sure to use a fire-safe container and proper safety procedures. In this way you will be releasing those worries to the universe and the universe will do with them as it sees fit. In the meantime, you are free from the burden of carrying them around in your mind.

Introduction to Advocacy

An advocate is a person or group of people who act to support a particular cause, proposal, or policy. Sometimes advocates go through formal training programs and at other times they are thrown in the fire feet first. You most likely fall into the second group if you are anything like me.

You play an important role as your spouse's partner, interpreter, advocate, and support. To do your best work you need to understand what is going on. Laying in a hospital bed with an illness/injury you have no control over, mourning the loss of a limb, and contemplating the uncertainty of your future, is terrifying. Your life is in the hands of a group of strangers who may or may not be at the top of their game. While it seems like you are carrying enough burden/responsibility to sink an elephant and your spouse is just lying there in the hospital, it is important to note that their mind is not at its peak. As they lay there surrounded by machines, being given drugs, and meeting doctor after doctor while undergoing more tests than they can count, their mind is overwhelmed with "what-ifs" and worse case scenarios. To be honest, if your spouse is like mine, within minutes of the doctor leaving the room your spouse will turn to you and ask what the doctor had just said. Our minds try to protect us by shutting down when they become overloaded. This means your spouse will often be so wrapped up in what is happening that they cannot absorb new information. If you have a solid understanding of what has been said, then you can relay it to your spouse in manageable bites that he can mentally handle. My preferred method is to consult a medical dictionary, medical terminology textbook, and anatomy charts. Then I translate what the doctor had said into English (because I wrote it down and asked him to spell anything I didn't know). When the diagnosis is complicated I will have a nurse read it against what their computer says to make sure my translation is accurate. Then I have Jason ask me specific questions he has and I answer them based on what I learned.

When your spouse is in the hospital they will be cared for by a multitude of doctors, nurses, transporters, aids, and technicians. Your spouse's records will be logged in his chart (or if your hospital has modernized they will be put in a computer system) where they can be accessed to varying degrees by each professional who will interact with your spouse. This gives the illusion of a well-oiled machine. The truth is that if you were to pull back that ugly room dividing curtain you will see that what you perceived to be a well-oiled machine is really several machines that just happen to be in sync. Each member of your spouse's care team is focused on their piece of the puzzle. Your responsibility is to keep track of all of those pieces and to make sure the puzzle is coming together.

Everyone on your spouse's care team is a human with a life of their own. They may really enjoy helping others heal but at the end of the day they are performing a job. They punch the time clock just as any waitress, factory worker, or a mechanic does. Now don't get me wrong, healthcare professionals do have a specific skill set that saves lives, literally. These people sacrifice sleep, family time, social lives, birthdays, holidays, etc. to care for complete strangers. But at the end of the day it is important to remember that they are human. They follow rules and directives handed down from their superiors and maybe more importantly, they are managing care for many people at the same time. While most of the time care is smoothly transitioned between shifts and a myriad of personnel, it is also important to be on guard for gaps. There have been times where we have had two different transporters show up to take my husband to two different tests regarding different symptoms in different parts of the hospital at the same time. We had to call in a doctor to decide which test to prioritize.

I once took Jason to the hospital because he was hemorrhaging instead of having actual bowel movements. We were in the emergency room for 2 hours. During that time, he made seven trips to the bathroom. Not once did a medical professional observe his output for diagnosis or treatment. Bloodwork was done and we were told that hemoglobin levels should be around 15. His were 12.8 and they would use that as a baseline. The doctor then prescribed him a medication to take that I recognized as one of the medications he cannot take so I brought it up to the doctor. It turns out she had no clue he was even on medications. Nobody bothered to ask about his medicines or medical history. If I hadn't been on my game, he could have been given a potentially fatal drug combination.

The symptoms didn't go away but the bleeding stopped temporarily. A few days later we had to admit him into the larger hospital, where he receives most of his care, due to increasingly disturbing symptoms. He hadn't been feeling well since he left the emergency room days prior so the night before this second trip to the hospital he had eaten less than 2 ounces of chicken and about a quarter of a cup of rice for dinner. He had skipped breakfast the day he was admitted because we had an early appointment to get to. After his appointment we stopped for lunch and before he could eat he almost collapsed. I immediately drove him to the hospital where he was admitted. His care team immediately got to work trying to stabilize his condition and get answers. At this time, they were unaware of the last time he had eaten nor were they concerned about it. Jason wasn't hungry. His health was more important.

If you have ever been admitted to the hospital or been with your spouse when he was admitted, you know that as soon as they are stabilized the protocol is to restrict food and drinks so doctors can order tests as needed. Jason did undergo various tests that evening which meant he wasn't able to eat at all that day because tests happened during meal times and the contrast dyes caused nausea. At midnight he was put on a "no food" restriction so he would be ready for new tests in the morning. Day two began with more testing, a lot of testing, causing him to miss both breakfast and lunch. For dinner he was restricted to one cup of beef broth and one snack cup of Jell-O. Midnight again brought a "no food" restriction. By dinner time on day three we had no answers and Jason was starving. In a 96-hour period he had consumed only 366 calories. He was both nauseous and famished. He needed food. His medical staff had no clue and had once again put him on a "no food" restriction for more tests. They were determined to find answers to his symptoms which seemed to be getting worse. Due to lack of nutrition he was struggling to think clearly and forming sentences was a struggle. He asked me to help. From the healthcare team's perspective, it looked as though Jason had been eating all along. He was allowed each meal and only restricted overnight. There were no detailed notes showing that he was missing meals due to the tests and the side effects of these tests. After his request, I tracked down a nurse and asked to speak with the doctor. It took a while for the doctor to become available but when we did see him I explained how long Jason had gone without food and that he needed to eat. The doctor was able to arrange a solid meal of meatloaf and mashed potatoes that helped Jason physically and mentally. They then placed a chart on his door to monitor his food intake for the rest of his stay.

If you see something not working or your spouse has a valid complaint, be sure to clearly communicate this concern to his care team. Also if your spouse has a legitimate request for a specific treatment or test and the doctor refuses to pursue it without a valid reason then request that the refusal be documented in his charts. Get a copy of that written refusal as well. Due to HIPAA laws you will not be able to make this request but your spouse has a legal right to all information in his case file, so they should be the one asking for the copy.

It is good to remember that doctors are human. They sometimes forget that medical terminology and human anatomy are not on everyone's curriculum vitae. If you have a basic understanding of medical terminology you may not understand exactly what was said but you can somewhat appreciate the fact that those mile-long words they use are meant to provide clarity in medical situations and not to sound pedantic and important. There are definitely times when I would rather hear there are swollen lymph nodes inside my husband's lungs causing his difficulty with breathing instead of "pulmonary lesions" and it is much easier on my frazzled mind to learn they are cutting off his leg below the knee as opposed to being told they will be performing a "trans-tibial amputation of the right leg". I strongly recommend getting your hands on a medical terminology book and maybe also an anatomy and physiology book. Do yourself a favor though and don't buy them from a bookstore. You will end up frustrated beyond belief. What you want is the textbook form. They can be found used at thrift stores, college bookstores, and online. These ones will be the easiest to understand and often include explanatory graphics to aid comprehension.

Clear communication with healthcare staff also means asking questions. Never feel stupid or like a burden when you don't understand what a doctor is saying or what a test result means. Each profession has its own jargon and sometimes professionals within that field forget that their knowledge is not common knowledge. You are all on the same team and your spouse's doctors are obligated to make sure your spouse knows fully what is being done to him, what he needs to do for his self, and the potential outcomes, both good and bad. Answers to your questions could be the difference between health and illness, life and death. Remember that the doctor is just a person in a white coat who happens to have specialized knowledge of the human condition. While he may seem brilliant in a hospital setting he would most likely feel inferior if asked to perform payroll duties, replace the intake valve on a semi-truck, bake a pecan pie, or whatever it is you specialize in. As the saying goes...*if you judge a fish by his ability to climb a tree it will spend its entire life believing it is stupid.* **Ask those questions. Question everything.**

Make sure you really know what's what, don't blindly trust that everything will work out.

You may also want to ask questions regarding the doctor's experience working with your spouse's particular medical needs. Some doctor's get a bit testy when their experience is questioned but if you do it with tact not too many feathers will get ruffled.

Like many people, I once believed that all doctors were trained the same way. I knew there were specialists such as dentists, podiatrists, and surgeons but I guess I had just assumed that all doctors received the same education and then chose to specialize afterward. To be honest, I am not sure that I really thought about this much at all.

Here's the scoop on doctors...they are not all the same. Even if they all had the same initial training, after years of working in a particular specialty they may forget the training that doesn't pertain to their current situation. More important for you to know is that experience is as important as knowledge. Unfortunately, amputees are a minority and amputations are not something every doctor is experienced or knowledgeable about. It is important to have professionals on the care team that have direct experience and knowledge of the special needs of amputees.

We learned this lesson by trial and error. After Jason's foot had been amputated across the arch, we were told to watch for redness as its presence would indicate that the blood supply was again impaired and medical intervention would be necessary. Now here's a fun fact---the entire surgical site is red after surgery. Go figure. Even though I diligently photographed the surgical site daily (I highly recommend doing this). I didn't understand exactly what I was watching for as I have never taken medically-oriented classes. It just so happens that pain is a side effect of compromised blood flow and it was this increasing pain that landed us back in the emergency room seeking solutions. The emergency doctor examined Jason's surgical site and said it appeared to be healing fine. He attributed the pain to the healing process, offered pain management medications, and sent us on our way. I took a few photos of his surgical site while it was un-bandaged, waited for it to be re-bandaged, and we went home breathing a little easier because we believed the doctor when he said that Jason's foot was healthy. Our biggest fear was a second surgery and removal of his leg below the knee. So far so good though. Fingers crossed, and all that jazz.

The very next day after this emergency room visit Jason had a previously scheduled appointment with his vascular surgeon. His vascular surgeon took one look at the surgical site and matter-of-factly announced that the foot was dying and further surgery would be necessary to save his quality of life. I insisted that we had done everything right and questioned how his foot could have died in less than 24 hours. The doctor looked at me confused so I explained how we had been in the emergency room just the day before and were told that his foot was healing well. I even had pictures to prove it. I showed the doctor the photos I had taken and he promptly pointed out where exactly it was dying. He also let us in on a secret...few doctors beyond those who specialize in amputations have any clue about the process, needs, care, or appearance of a healing amputation site.

This incident also taught me the importance of clarification. Had I probed the doctor more about what "red" meant then maybe I would have better understood what I was looking for. In Jason's case, his arteries had closed again which diminished blood flow to the foot so even if I had known what "red" meant and he would have gotten proper medical intervention the day before in the emergency room, the result would have been the same. His only option was to amputate above the damaged arteries. There are many instances though where delayed treatment/intervention could cause great risk. So it is important to always make sure you know what to look for, how to properly care for the wound, and if your spouse ever tells you something doesn't seem right, take them seriously. Your spouse may not know what is wrong or be able to describe it in a logical manner but that won't make it any less true. Remember, your spouse is the only true expert on his body. It is always better to get the situation assessed by professionals and have it be nothing than it is to ignore the signs/symptoms and have it be something.

While we are focusing on the things doctors overlook or don't always remember, there will be times that you will be asked to perform wound care for your spouse. Doctors are so used to being elbow deep in bodily fluids that they don't always realize how gross that is to the rest of us. In the past three years I have been asked to insert three feet of gauze into a tunnel the size of a dime in the end of my husband's stump, empty bodily fluids from a vacuum pump, clean surgical sites, and more. Now, as much as I would like to say that as a dutiful wife I happily did all that for him. The truth is that I drew deep lines in the sand as to what I was willing to do and what I wasn't. In my many decades of life I had been acclimated to bodily fluids, bandaging a variety of wounds, and other basic first aid activities but at no time had I ever had to insert anything into someone and I wasn't about to do it now.

We were in a wound care clinic and I had just watched the doctor pack three feet of gauze into a tunnel that had developed in Jason's stump. Then without warning he turned to me with a second jar of gauze and told me that on Saturday he wanted me to remove the current gauze pack and to use a skewer to repack the tunnel. I looked him dead in the eye and said 'no.' The expression on his face said quite clearly that he wasn't used to being told no when he instructed patients and their spouses in wound care, but I wasn't doing it. We have children and pets. Our house is far from sterile and I am not taking on the responsibility of potentially packing Jason's already impaired limb with bacteria which would lead to further issues. After the doctor's confused expression subsided I explained that I did not feel comfortable doing a procedure like that on anyone but I would be willing to bring him back down to the clinic to have it repacked. After a little song and dance it was decided that the doctor didn't want to work on Saturday and that Jason would be fine if the gauze was removed on Saturday and the wound covered until the doctor could pack it on Monday. **The moral of this story is this... know your limits. Never do (or agree to do) anything that you are uncomfortable performing, don't fully understand, or that you feel has a large margin for error. They are the healthcare providers, not you. They went to medical school, not you. Your job is to provide emotional support, love, and basic physical support to your spouse in their time of need. Medical intervention is not a skill that can be learned on the fly. Refusing to do medical procedures you are not knowledgeable about and that you feel uncomfortable with does not diminish what you bring to the table.**

If you have not been formally trained in the medical procedure you are being asked to perform (or even if you have but you don't feel confident about your abilities) and you feel uncomfortable performing it, tell the doctor immediately. You are not responsible for performing medical procedures no matter how minor they may seem. There is always the possibility of something going sideways and the result could be great harm to your spouse. Individuals with M.D., R.N., and other alphabet soups related to human health DO NOT have the authority to deputize you in performing medical interventions no matter how trivial the procedure may seem. Know your limits and advocate for the care that is best for your spouse.

Your advocacy duties don't end when your spouse leaves the hospital. This will be a long-term position that you will continue to hold. While they may be in a better place mentally once they have left the hospital, sometimes they aren't. Three years out of surgery, my husband struggles with his mental wounds as much as he does his physical wounds. He is not always capable of explaining to medical personnel what he is experiencing and the kind of help he is seeking and I am left pick up the gauntlet and make sure he is getting what he needs.

Being an advocate for your spouse isn't always easy. And trust me, there are times when it seems like his medical team is plotting against you. It isn't true but there are times when it feels that way. We were two and a half months into our amputation journey. By this time Jason had undergone two angioplasties, a clot removal surgery, and the amputation of half of his foot. These measures had proven unsuccessful and surgery was scheduled for the trans-tibial amputation of his leg, just above the clotting arteries. We were nervous and excited about what this would mean to our family. On the Friday afternoon before his Wednesday surgery I received a phone call from the hospital. It had only come to their attention at that moment that his primary care doctor was in another town and didn't have practicing rights at the hospital where the surgery would take place. Because the rest of his procedures were done on an emergency basis or as an outpatient, it had never been an issue. So here I am at 2:00pm on a Friday afternoon and the woman on the other end of the phone is telling me that I have until Tuesday afternoon to find my husband a local doctor and to get him a surgery clearance or his surgery would be postponed and the next available date could be as long as a month away. His foot was dying. The pain was excruciating and most likely if his surgery was postponed he would find himself receiving emergency surgery for gangrene well before the next scheduled date. I couldn't let this happen.

When I hung up the phone, I immediately called his insurance provider for a list of physicians that accept his insurance. Then I began calling them all. For anyone who has ever tried to be a new patient somewhere, you well know that new patient appointments are scheduled two to three months out. This is exactly what I had encountered. After the third call I was running out of time and was feeling the pressure so I changed up my technique. Instead of asking if they were accepting new patients and continuing with the same old song and dance, my phone calls went a bit like this, "Hello, my husband is scheduled for a life-saving lower extremity amputation on Wednesday, August 24th. The hospital performing the surgery just informed me that because his current doctor is affiliated with a different hospital and cannot practice at the one doing the procedure that I have until Tuesday August 23rd to get established with a new doctor AND have a surgery clearance exam performed or they will cancel and reschedule his surgery. This means that he will not only suffer excruciating pain but will most likely suffer complications from the already developing gangrene on his foot. Is there a doctor who could possibly help us out?"

I won't lie, I received a lot of "no" answers. I actually expected as much. I was searching for a minnow in an ocean of fish. But our story stuck in the mind of one of the people who I talked to and she actually called me back to tell me of an urgent care doctor who once had stepped up as the surgical clearance doctor for a boy with special needs who required dental surgery. She gave me his information and said to give it a try. I did put in a call to them and was awaiting a return call when I tried one more number. It was a clinic but worth a shot. They were so eager to help us keep our surgery date that they contacted one of their physician's assistants that was on vacation (a staycation actually) to see if she would be able to come in for an hour and perform his surgical clearance for us since all of the other staff were booked solid. And that is exactly what this wonderful woman did. We met her on Monday and got confirmation of his clearance the same day.

The moral of the story is to be persistent when all hope is lost. Don't be afraid to share your story. Doctor offices receive calls every day from people who believe exceptions should be made for them to be seen sooner or granted other special treatments. Emergency rooms and urgent cares were created to support the often hectic and full schedules of the primary care physicians. But there are times when extenuating circumstances must be considered. If being seen immediately by a specific professional could prevent a negative outcome to a life or death situation, share your story and make it happen.

I do believe that I found success in getting my husband the clearance he needed for two reasons. The first being that I refused to give up. If someone couldn't help me, I asked if they knew someone who may be able to. The second reason is because I didn't demand that anyone help me. Nor did I assume they would. I simply stated our predicament and asked if there was anyone available to help us. If the answer was no, I thanked them and moved on.

Write it Down

Medical emergencies can be stressful. It isn't possible to remember everything. For this reason, I like to carry a small notebook around to write down what the doctor says so that I can remember it when necessary. Always remember to write down who said it and the date they said it on. Trust me, you will not remember this later.

If your spouse was your main or sole income, you could also find yourself contacting agencies to help with necessities such as rental payments, medical bills, utility payments, and food. When you fall down this rabbit hole everything will begin to blend together and you will soon forget who offers what, which places you contacted, and how you learned of them. For this reason, I have included this little cheat sheet that you can photocopy and use as needed.

These notes will come in handy when you sit down to write thank you notes. They will also save you precious time if you've properly logged who you talked to, the date you talked to them, and what help they did and can offer. You'll be able to flip through your notes instead of wracking your brain or starting all over with the phone calls.

In a perfect world, your spouse would undergo amputation, heal beautifully and quickly, get a prosthetic, and walk back into life. The reality is that the healing process is slow and even under the most ideal circumstances there will be setbacks. As I talked about before, it is important to be prepared. Over the years I have used folders and 3-ring binders to organize the piles of paperwork. Last year I created the ultimate binder. The cover is made of two sturdy clipboards that are bound together with construction grade u-clips. This binder holds a whopping 500 sheets of paper. As you can imagine this can be quite cumbersome to carry around so it is important to also carry a Cliff's notes version. For us it's a small notebook that tracks current medications, recent surgeries and procedures, and health issues. This is easier to carry along and can be a big help when your mind is preoccupied with whatever medical emergency has brought you two into the hospital. The key is to remember to update it every time there is a change. I find that it is easiest to update it in real life. When you are waiting to be seen after a fall, jot that down. When your spouse is hospitalized, write down the pertinent details while sitting next to his bed. Memory is fickle and untrustworthy. Write it down.

My organized Organizations
(Photocopy this page if you need more than what is provided.)

- Organization Name:
- How I learned of this Organization:
- Department/Contact Person:
- Phone Number:
- Mailing Address:
- Email:
- Fax:
- Hours of Operation/ Days:
- Specific Help Provided:
- Requirements to receive Aid:
- Date Help was Received:
- Type/Amount of help Received:
- How often this Help is available:

Meeting the Experts

During your spouse's many medical appointments and hospitalizations you both will encounter a myriad of professionals with degrees in internal medicine, nursing, surgical studies, specific organ systems, counseling, etc. They have studied their chosen field and met the criteria to qualify for certification/licensing and the right to practice their preferred type of medicine. But there will also be two experts on the scene who will be overlooked often because they don't have an alphabet of credentials behind their name, no formal training in medicine, and no prestigious white coat. Those experts are you and your spouse. Read that again. Those experts are you and your spouse. That's right. Despite their years of study and practice, doctors and nurses come in third when vying for the position of top experts on your spouse. They have been trained in procedures. They have studied how particular medicines and procedures affect the general population undergoing them. Your spouse is the only one who truly knows their body, how it reacts to pain, how it feels, what medications work, and their abilities and limitations. You have an intimate knowledge of your spouse and a less biased understanding of these facets of your spouse. For instance, you have the ability to sense changes in his/her behavior that may indicate pain or discomfort, changes in speech that may indicate an impending issue, changes in a wound or skin color that aren't significant enough to be noticed by medical professionals. **I cannot emphasize enough how important it is for the two of you to become advocates for your spouse's care. If either of you feel something wrong is being overlooked or medical wishes are going unmet, or the side effects of a medication are too much it is imperative for you to speak up. You are the expert here.** You both are important members of your care team and should be treated as such. You are paying for this team either out of pocket or through insurance premiums and have the right to fire anyone who is not working in your spouse's best interest. And you have the right to know what all test results are and the details of all treatments and procedures...IN PLAIN ENGLISH.

Years ago Jason when hospitalized after suffering the diabetic coma described earlier. He spent a week in the hospital and nurses woke him periodically through the night to do his blood draws for testing. A few days into his stay he told me that they kept waking him every few hours for blood draws but nobody would tell him why they were taking blood and what the results were. I went to the nurse desk and asked that we be updated immediately of what was being tested and what was found. The first time I was giving a pat response that someone would be in shortly. When that didn't happen I asked another nurse. It took me three nurses but the third one came in with Jason's binder and went through every test and the results. She then told us she would be working the rest of his week-long stay and would come in every morning to update us on every test he had undergone and that is exactly what she did. The key is to be persistent.

You also have the right to obtain copies of your medical records. Often there is a charge for these services. Our hospital system charges $2.00 the first page and $1.00 each additional page. When you're hospitalized for a week or more and have had surgeries and tests and procedures, it is easy to stack up thousands of pages in your file. Our hospital will ask specifically what you want...the entire file, only surgical notes, test results, medication notes, etc. They also offer a service that allows you to get the entire file on a compact disc for $5.00 which is by far the best deal. The drawback is you will need to have a computer to access them. To be honest, you won't understand even a fraction of what is in that file nor are you expected to. The reason for collecting these discs of hospital stays is to provide comprehensive care.

Our hospital has a network of several hospitals in seven or eight different counties. They also operate various primary care offices, blood labs, and urgent cares. All of these services are linked by a central computer network known as EPIC so that if my husband were to go to urgent care in the network complaining of pain or heat in a wound and was told to go to the hospital, he won't have to waste time repeating what's wrong, they will be able to bring his chart up immediately and see what was tried already and/or diagnosed. If we were to be on vacation and something happened to send him to the hospital, they would have no idea about what he has been through and what his medical history is. These records on disc allow you to update doctors with historically accurate information and more details than you could have given yourself.

During my husband's follow-up after his first amputation the tech did a vascularity test of his leg. At the end he printed out the results and I asked for a copy. He was confused and he asked if I wanted the print out or if I wanted the findings after they had been read. I explained I wanted a photocopy of the pages in his hand to which he retorted that I wouldn't understand them. I countered by explaining that I don't need to understand them, that I want to have them in hand in case we find ourselves in another hospital so the doctors can see where he was on a specific date and create a baseline. He was more than willing to provide me with a copy.

The Illusion of Freedom and the sliding scale of ability

The amputee life is unpredictable. More so than life with a toddler. One day everything can be great and your spouse could climb a mountain and the next day he could be so swollen that he can't even get his prosthetic on. As easy as it is to give trite advice like "learn to roll with the punches" and "expect the unexpected", the truth is that no matter how prepared you think you are, something new is going to come along and throw you for a loop.

The best thing you can do is to face your greatest fear and make a contingency plan for it. Then if things go sideways you can always look back at this guide and remind yourself that you've got this.

Each person's worst case scenario may be different. For one it may be the death of their spouse. For another it may be if their spouse can no longer work. And in all honesty, your worst case scenario can change over time so you can fill out this worksheet as often as you need to.

Worst Case Scenario

- What is the current situation?
- What is the worst possible outcome that could happen?
- If the worst case scenario were to happen, what are three small things you could do to stabilize the situation?
- Who are three people who could help you immediately?
- What are 5 things you can do right now to prepare for this worst case scenario?
- What is the outcome I am hoping for?
- What are the 5 things I can do right now to influence a positive outcome?
- Who are 3 people who could help me positively influence this situation?

It is true that now that your spouse is an amputee your spouse won't be able to do everything that he once did. There will be times when he truly cannot do basic activities and will need your help. But there will also be times when it will appear that he can conquer the world. There won't be any rhyme or reason to what he is capable of on any particular day so you need to look at it all with an attitude of "it is what it is".

One day, not too long ago, my husband and I took our youngest son on a trek through the woods. We walked a mile path, climbing over fallen trees, navigating uneven terrain, and trying not to stumble over unearthed roots. Afterward, my husband felt good and his leg looked great. A week or so later we had gone to a public park. While there, my husband walked a short ¼ mile along a paved path, resting a few times along the way. When we got home we realized he had developed a large blister across the bottom of his stump and he ended up out of commission for almost 4 weeks.

When your spouse first receives his amputation, there is a healing process that renders them unable to care for themselves. In many cases this is an extended period and the spouse often takes on the caretaker role. I hear it quite a bit from caretakers that they feel they now have another child and wish that their spouse would do more for himself. When asked why they keep doing for him the answer is usually something along the lines of "I have just become used to doing it." Instead of growing resentful from doing everything, memorize and use this one sentence, "can you do this yourself or do you need my help?". There will be days when he can do the things and others when he can't.

I also recommend filling in the following chart. It will benefit both of you as you will have a visual reminder that just because he cannot do all of the things, he can still do some of the things.

Things he can no longer do:

Things he can do with assistance:

Things he can do with accommodation:

Things he can absolutely do:

Re-evaluate this list often as everything can change from day to day.

All throughout the amputation process it seems as though a prosthetic limb is the holy grail. After all, a prosthetic limb is the key to mobility and returning to life as you once knew it. This is a formula for disappointment. In full disclosure, I have met amputees that have returned

What Really Matters

Before your spouse becomes an amputee, your priorities may look different than they will after the amputation. Prior to whatever medical emergency has affected your family, you probably led a full life filled with work, family, friends, events, bills, hobbies, etc. During the medical emergency most of these priorities likely faded into oblivion due to shifting needs, time constraints, new responsibilities, and pure exhaustion. This new set of priorities may follow you in the weeks and months that follow the hospitalization. Eventually the dust will settle though and decisions must be made. Will you continue on with these new priorities or will you return to the life you once lived (with some MAJOR accommodations, trust me on this one)?

If there is a significant difference between your before and after priorities, there can be a strong pull in both directions. This will be especially true where people are involved. Friends, family members, and co-workers may not understand decisions you are now making regarding how you spend your time and money. That's okay. It's not your job to lead them to understanding. The important thing is that you are doing what is best for your family.

After Jason underwent amputation, our priorities changed. His desire to work 60+ hours a week was replaced by the realization of how much he had missed in his children's lives by working so much. During the three months between his first and final amputations he grew accustomed to seeing them all the time, listening to how their day went at school, and meeting their friends. For this reason, he decided that if ever he reached a point in his recovery that he could return to work he would no longer work evenings or weekends. That time would be for his family.

Another priority that changed for us was our overall life goals. Until this medical emergency had occurred, I had never wanted to own a home. I enjoyed the luxury of being able to relocate when I wanted to and the freedom from the cost of large repairs. Jason on the other hand, wanted to buy a large home. Something that could accommodate long visits from children and grandchildren. This changed when we found ourselves homeless because we no longer met the minimum income requirements to renew our lease (even though we were current on all payments).

Being an amputee is difficult. It takes more effort both mentally and physically to get around whether you use crutches, a cane, a wheelchair, or a prosthetic. The shear exhaustion Jason experiences trying to navigate from the living room to the bathroom in our 900 square foot home has shrank the size of his dream house. Together we decided that our ideal home would be a 600 square foot cabin with an open floorplan and step-free entrance.

While we are currently renting while we pay off a few medical and student loan bills, we will one day be able to buy a house that fits our needs. I add this for others who find themselves with extremely low incomes that wish they could be a homeowner. With a little research I was able to learn that USDA has a Home Loan program with a zero down option. It is available for anyone who doesn't already own an adequate home and those who make 115% or less of the area's median income. Essentially there are two programs. The first is a mortgage through a traditional lender that is guaranteed by USDA for up to 90% of the purchase price. The second is for extremely low income households (this is where those living solely on disability payments would qualify) and the mortgage is handled 100% by the USDA. It may be something to look into, especially if you are a renter in a home that isn't handicap accessible.

Due to other health issues and complications of his amputation, Jason was declared disabled. This single designation led to a chain reaction of changes in our lives that we never could have imagined. Because we were no longer working traditional jobs (he was disabled and I was a non-paid caregiver for him), we were considered to be out of the rat race. We lost quite a few friends at this time who apparently felt that our only connection was a shared financial struggle. Which is quite ironic considering we were struggling at a level most have never known to exist. Others fell out of our lives because they were uncomfortable with the rawness of our situation or because we could no longer do for them what they had become accustomed to. At times those losses hurt but looking back it turned out to be just fine. The lesson is to focus on what is most important to your family. It doesn't matter if others don't understand or approve of your new life. They don't have to live with your choices, you do. In our experience, when the fair-weather friends fade away, new friends will step up and bring a refreshing lightness to your lives.

The Responsibility Pyramid

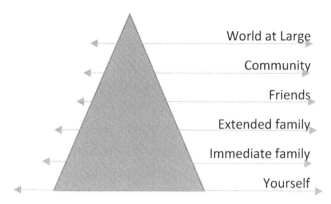

In marriages the workload is often divided. Sometimes the division is even with both working, caring for the children, and maintaining the house. Other times the responsibilities are doled out based on each person's strengths and preferences. Each couple must decide what works for them.

This may sound weird or selfish but I would like you to look at the responsibility pyramid above. Note that the largest portion is dedicated for yourself, the smallest for the world-at-large, and everyone else falls somewhere in between. There is a good reason for this. While your life may have seemed hectic before the medical emergency, the chaos will grow to epic proportions and I cannot express strongly enough how important it is for you to take care of yourself. With that said, let's look at responsibilities.

What must be done before a medical emergency may look much different than what must be done during the medical emergency and what you must do afterward. Please note that while the word 'emergency' usually refers to a single moment in time when someone needs assistance and usually lasts under a few hours, here it is expanded from the moment the decision to amputate is made, through the amputation, and to the end of the recovery period. For some this may take months, for others it can be years or decades.

If you refer to the responsibility pyramid, you will remember that your greatest responsibility will be to yourself. If you go down, everything falls apart really quick. Like Flash Gordon running quick. Like blink of an eye quick. The speed at which all those balls you've been juggling fall to the ground is astonishing to say the least. So make sure you are feeding yourself properly, getting adequate rest, and staying hydrated.

Your next responsibility is to your children. They depend on you for so much of their safety, health, and mental/physical well-being and you must continue to provide them that security and refuge. When it comes to children, especially those under age 13, try to keep their routines, meals, and bedtimes as normal as possible. You may have to delegate grandma to take your oldest to karate class but the important part is that they got to go.

Also make time to attend any function where your child will be recognized for their achievement. Kids are often self-centric but they do see what's going on around them. When one parent is in the hospital and facing a life altering surgery, they need that reassurance that the other parent is going to be there for them no matter how inconvenient or minimal it may be in the grand scheme of things. They need to know that if their fears come true that they can depend on you. Most importantly, make time to have fun with your kids. This doesn't have to require money (Lord knows there isn't much of that around at this time). The following is a list of activities you can do with your kids that require minimal amounts of energy on your part.

- Blowing bubbles
- Watching a movie with yummy snacks
- Baking cookies
- A bike ride
- Nature walk
- Drawing/coloring
- Painting
- Making up a story
- Playing in a sprinkler
- Building a snowman
- Reading a book
- Building with Legos
- Building a blanket fort

After you have met the needs of yourself and your children, the next person on the list is your spouse. Now it may seem illogical to put your spouse third on the list so let me explain. Your spouse is most likely in a hospital or care center at this time. He has 24-hour access, 7 days a week, to people who will meet his every need. All his meals are delivered to him, he can get assistance with toileting and showering if necessary, and he has a television all to himself with every choice of program cable has to offer. There are people to adjust the thermostat, bring him blankets, make his bed, take him for walks, and fulfill his every need. Yes, he may prefer YOU do these things. Yes, he may desperately need to be physically close to you and have someone he can talk to. But he doesn't have to be alone when you aren't there. He can contact friends and family to arrange visits to keep his spirits up. The reason he comes in third in this pyramid is mainly because if you are sick, even if you do manage to drag your sick self to the hospital, on many of the floors he would be on you would be denied access due to the likelihood of you infecting your spouse or other patients. And if your children are so discombobulated that they are having meltdowns and are unable to be consoled, you won't be able to find anyone to watch them so you can get to the hospital anyway.

The last group is really a compilation of all the rest of the pyramid. This includes extended family, friends, co-workers, bosses, and everyone else you encounter on a regular basis. These people, are on the pyramid only because before this medical emergency you may have had a multitude of obligations to them. In the midst of a medical emergency whether it be the amputation itself or a hospitalization for other issues, the people who fall into this list should be able to realize that they need to find someone else to tend to their problems/needs. Do not feel obligated to stretch yourself too thin doing stuff for this group.

When it comes to your boss and job, you will need to find the balance that works for you. In my opinion, being there for my spouse during a hospitalization is more important than any task at work whether I am flipping burgers or overseeing daily operations of a Fortune 500 company. But each person needs to decide for themselves how this division of responsibility will look.

When Jason initially went into the hospital my to-do list didn't disappear and I would think it a safe bet that neither will yours. Some of these tasks will demand to be done such as car maintenance, house maintenance, laundry, grocery shopping, etc. Other things can be let go. One night while I was particularly stressed I created what I call my To-Don't list. It looks like a to-do list but works in an opposite way. Think of it as your To-do list's evil twin. I still use this list all these years later. Whenever I find something that has been on my to-do list for a few weeks and I just really don't want to do it I ask myself if not doing it will matter a year from now. If the answer is 'no' then I add it to my To-Don't list and cross if off the to-do list. While the idea may sound crazy, it is actually great for the mental health. By moving it to the To-Don't list, it is still there if you ever decide to do it but it frees up space on your to-do list for more important tasks. I recommend these to everyone.

Simple ways to Nurture your Relationships

The slope from spouse to caregiver brings with it many challenges but there are also many ways to maintain your original relationship and nurture the love that initially brought you together. The following list should get you started. But please note that these must go both ways. If you are constantly giving and never receiving your cup will soon empty and nothing will be gained.

- Stop overanalyzing flaws
- Choose to be supportive
- Happy spouse, happy house
- Ask for dream updates
- Never underestimate the power of love
- Don't let your children come between you
- Stop questioning motives
- Graciously receive compliments
- Let go of your top three pet peeves
- Predict the predictable and make peace with it
- Use letters as a communication tool
- Gracefully accept apologies
- Practice regular stress prevention
- Don't speak for others
- Stop being demanding

- Practice unconditional love
- Say "I'm sorry"
- Stay away from comparisons
- Remember the magic
- Learn to laugh at yourself
- Let it go already
- Throw away the scoreboard
- Be kind first
- Express love
- Look for the gifts
- Take perspective
- Stay away from ultimatums
- Allow time for transitions
- Put a positive spin on things
- Set a good example
- Become a world-class listener
- Focus on the important stuff
- Stop wishing s/he was different
- Think before you speak
- What are you contributing to the problem
- Fulfill the promise
- Think gentle thoughts
- Stay compassionate
- Don't allow passing thoughts to turn into issues
- Become a low-maintenance partner
- Do your relationship your way
- Choose peace over irritation

- Stay playful
- Stop rehearsing unhappiness
- Don't be the hero in every story
- Sit in silence
- Take responsibility for your own happiness
- Stop being so defensive
- Be grateful
- Respond with love

So there you have it! The guide that I wish I had had when we started on this path. I hope you have found it to be helpful. Every experience is different but know that there are people out there who are rooting for you to succeed down this road.

Jason Andrew Whitney.

Man. Myth. Legend.

This last chapter is dedicated to my husband and all of the amputee spouses out there. Throughout this book I have talked in depth about the stresses, obstacles, frustrations, and nuances of caring for an amputee. Now I would like to take a moment to give you some insight into this same life from an amputee viewpoint.

For many years now, I have watched this man change. He has good days and bad days and either can stretch into weeks or months with no rhyme or reason. This is not the man that I once married. Physically he looks the same but his entire world, self-view, and perspectives have all changed.

As an amputee, there will be times we will plan outings, gatherings, or events only to find that we aren't able to go because he cannot get into his leg or his anxiety is off the charts. I can see the struggle in his eyes. There are always tears just waiting to flow if he ever let down his fight to hold them back. Most days he feels he is holding us back from enjoying life and living it up and he can't see why we would rather change our plans to keep him company.

For decades he has prided himself on working hard and providing for his family. He doesn't always say it but it tears him up inside to know that I now have to work and even then we struggle to stay afloat. He can't see that our needs are met and the only one who is resentful about our current finances is him.

Our children are a double edged sword to him. We have four children total ranging in age from 27 down to six years old. He worked long hours on nights and weekends which meant he missed watching the older two grow up and participating in their lives. Because of his amputation and poor health, he gets to enjoy the time he has with our younger two children. But there is always a cloud hanging over him, reminding him that if one of the boys were to get hurt under his watch or need saving, he wouldn't be able to get to them or remove them from the danger.

We never took many vacations. Actually, we never took ANY vacations when he was working. There was never time or money for such frivolities. With his amputation, our priorities changed and we try to take three to four vacations a year. Usually to natural places within a few hour drive of our home. We don't spend much but we always have a blast. He acts like it doesn't bother him but he is often hiding embarrassment and frustration when I call ahead to places to make sure he can access them. There are many times when he insists on staying in the car so we can see sights he cannot get to or experience events that would be too exhausting for him.

He doesn't see what he means to us anymore. Sometimes I wonder if all these years he thought I was only with him for his ability to earn an income. I don't really know.

Every aspect of our relationship has changed. In the beginning it seemed like it was all falling apart but now, looking back, I can see how much better we are.

It hasn't been easy but it has been a wild ride and if I could shout out to the world anything about Jason it would be this:

For all the frustrations, sleepless nights, wound care escapades, angry arguments, and major setbacks we have experienced, I am glad we went through them together. I have enjoyed all of those long drives to appointments where we were able to have deep conversations and enjoy the scenery. I love that we have transitioned from rushing everywhere to taking our time. It is wonderful to see you at school events for the boys. I am proud of how far you have come in your recovery and that you never gave up no matter what life threw at you. I admire the strength you have shown while experiencing excruciating long-term pain. Most of all, I am glad that you seek help when you need it now instead of pretending like everything will magically heal itself.

You are strong, brave, loving, funny, persistent, and humble. I am glad I have travelled this path by your side.

Resources

- Lost in Thought Project
- Facebook group: 'Spousal/Caregiver Of An Amputee Support Group' group
- Nike Reuse-A-Shoe program
- Amputee Coalition
- Army surplus stores carry special zippers with eyelets along the side. These zippers can be laced into work boots, hikers, and laced winter boots to turn them into a zippered boot so they are easier to get on and off the prosthetic foot.
- Department of Health and Human Services can help with a variety of services
- Local churches have resources to assist with food, gas cards, and certain car repairs
- State Disability Services

Made in the USA
Coppell, TX
01 July 2023

18681253R00059